KT-428-786

KEEP
CALM
FOR
CHAPS

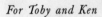

For Toby and Ken

KEEP CALM FOR CHAPS

GOOD ADVICE FOR HARD TIMES

EBURY
PRESS

1 3 5 7 9 10 8 6 4 2

This edition published 2011
First published in 2011 by Ebury Press, an imprint of Ebury Publishing
A Random House Group company

Compilation copyright © Ebury Press 2011

The Random House Group Limited Reg. No. 954009

Addresses for companies within the Random House Group can be found
at www.randomhouse.co.uk

A CIP catalogue record for this book is available from the British Library

The Random House Group Limited supports The Forest Stewardship
Council (FSC), the leading international forest certification organisation.
All our titles that are printed on Greenpeace approved FSC certified
paper carry the FSC logo. Our paper procurement policy can
be found at www.randomhouse.co.uk/environment

Designed and set by seagulls.net

Printed in Germany by GGP Media GmbH, Pössneck

ISBN 9780091943653

To buy books by your favourite authors and register for offers visit
www.randomhouse.co.uk

**COURAGE IS BEING
SCARED TO DEATH
– BUT SADDLING
UP ANYWAY.**

John Wayne

CONTENTS

Youth

Marriage

Fatherhood

Children

Middle Age

Money

Work

Home

Manners

Appearance

Bravery

Learning

Success

Adversity

Luck

Friendship
Enemies
Health
Sex
Exercise
Travel
Reflection
Opportunity
Relaxation
Temptation
The Future
Wisdom
Old Age
Life
Death

YOUTH

BOYHOOD, LIKE MEASLES, IS ONE OF THOSE COMPLAINTS WHICH A MAN SHOULD CATCH YOUNG AND HAVE DONE WITH, FOR WHEN IT COMES IN MIDDLE LIFE IT IS APT TO BE SERIOUS.

P G Wodehouse

KEEP TRUE TO THE DREAMS OF YOUR YOUTH.

Friedrich Schiller

TOO CHASTE A YOUTH LEADS TO A DISSOLUTE OLD AGE.

André Gide

MARRIAGE

AN OBJECT IN POSSESSION SELDOM RETAINS THE SAME CHARM THAT IT HAD IN PURSUIT.

Pliny the Younger

WHEN A MAN STEALS YOUR WIFE, THERE IS NO BETTER REVENGE THAN TO LET HIM KEEP HER.

Sacha Guitry

GIVE UP ALL
HOPE OF PEACE
SO LONG AS YOUR
MOTHER-IN-LAW
IS ALIVE.

Juvenal

NEVER MARRY
FOR MONEY.
YE'LL BORROW
IT CHEAPER.

Scottish proverb

FATHERHOOD

BECOMING A FATHER IS EASY ENOUGH, BUT BEING ONE CAN BE VERY ROUGH.

Wilhelm Busch

A FATHER IS A MAN WHO CARRIES A PICTURE OF HIS CHILDREN IN HIS WALLET WHERE HIS MONEY USED TO BE.

Anon

BY THE TIME A MAN REALIZES THAT MAYBE HIS FATHER WAS RIGHT, HE USUALLY HAS A SON WHO THINKS HE'S WRONG.

Charles Wadsworth

CHILDREN

**LEARNING TO
DISLIKE CHILDREN AT
AN EARLY AGE SAVES
A LOT OF EXPENSE
AND AGGRAVATION
LATER IN LIFE.**

Robert Byrne

NEVER RAISE YOUR HAND TO YOUR CHILDREN; IT LEAVES YOUR MIDSECTION UNPROTECTED.

Robert Orben

TO BRING UP A CHILD IN THE WAY HE SHOULD GO, TRAVEL THAT WAY YOURSELF ONCE IN A WHILE.

Josh Billings

CHILDREN ARE
A GREAT COMFORT
IN YOUR OLD AGE
– AND THEY HELP
YOU REACH IT
FASTER, TOO.

Lionel Kauffman

**YOU CAN LEARN
MANY THINGS FROM
CHILDREN. HOW
MUCH PATIENCE YOU
HAVE, FOR INSTANCE.**

Franklin P Jones

MIDDLE AGE

MIDDLE AGE IS WHEN YOU'RE SITTING AT HOME ON A SATURDAY NIGHT AND THE TELEPHONE RINGS AND YOU HOPE IT ISN'T FOR YOU.

Ogden Nash

BE WISE WITH SPEED;
A FOOL AT FORTY IS
A FOOL INDEED.

Edward Young

MIDDLE AGE IS THE TIME WHEN A MAN IS ALWAYS THINKING THAT IN A WEEK OR TWO HE WILL FEEL AS GOOD AS EVER.

Don Marquis

THE OLDER I GET THE BETTER I USED TO BE!

Lee Trevino

MONEY

MY PROBLEM LIES IN RECONCILING MY GROSS HABITS WITH MY NET INCOME.

Errol Flynn

A WISE MAN SHOULD HAVE MONEY IN HIS HEAD, BUT NOT IN HIS HEART.

Jonathan Swift

WHATEVER YOU HAVE, SPEND LESS.

Dr Johnson

IT IS BETTER TO HAVE A PERMANENT INCOME THAN TO BE FASCINATING.

Oscar Wilde

WORK

WHEN A MAN TELLS YOU THAT HE GOT RICH THROUGH HARD WORK, ASK HIM: 'WHOSE?'

Don Marquis

LIVE NEITHER IN THE PAST NOR IN THE FUTURE, BUT LET EACH DAY'S WORK ABSORB YOUR ENTIRE ENERGIES, AND SATISFY YOUR WIDEST AMBITION.

Sir William Osler

IF YOU THINK YOUR
BOSS IS STUPID,
REMEMBER: YOU
WOULDN'T HAVE
A JOB IF HE WAS
ANY SMARTER.

Albert A Grant

BY WORKING FAITHFULLY EIGHT HOURS A DAY, YOU MAY EVENTUALLY GET TO BE A BOSS AND WORK TWELVE HOURS A DAY.

Robert Frost

HOME

SHOW ME A
MAN WHO LIVES
ALONE AND HAS A
PERPETUALLY CLEAN
KITCHEN, AND
8 TIMES OUT OF 9 I'LL
SHOW YOU A MAN
WITH DETESTABLE
SPIRITUAL QUALITIES.

Charles Bukowski

**MANY A MAN WHO
THINKS TO FOUND
A HOME DISCOVERS
THAT HE HAS MERELY
OPENED A TAVERN
FOR HIS FRIENDS.**

Norman Douglas

DO YOU KNOW WHAT IT MEANS TO COME HOME AT NIGHT TO A WOMAN WHO'LL GIVE YOU A LITTLE LOVE, A LITTLE AFFECTION, A LITTLE TENDERNESS? IT MEANS YOU'RE IN THE WRONG HOUSE, THAT'S WHAT IT *MEANS*.

Henry Youngman

ONE ONLY NEEDS TWO TOOLS IN LIFE: WD-40 TO MAKE THINGS GO, AND DUCT TAPE TO MAKE THEM STOP.

G M Weilacher

MANNERS

A GENTLEMAN IS ANY MAN WHO WOULDN'T HIT A WOMAN WITH HIS HAT ON.

Fred Allen

A GENTLEMAN
CAN LIVE THROUGH
ANYTHING.

William Faulkner

MANNERS
MAKETH MAN.

William of Wykeham

THE ONLY INFALLIBLE RULE WE KNOW IS, THAT THE MAN WHO IS ALWAYS TALKING ABOUT BEING A GENTLEMAN NEVER IS ONE.

Robert Smith Surtees

APPEARANCE

EVERY UNIFORM CORRUPTS ONE'S CHARACTER.

Max Frisch

FASHION IS WHAT YOU ADOPT WHEN YOU DON'T KNOW WHO YOU ARE.

Quentin Crisp

BEWARE OF ALL ENTERPRISES THAT REQUIRE NEW CLOTHES.

Henry David Thoreau

BRAVERY

IT IS CURIOUS THAT PHYSICAL COURAGE SHOULD BE SO COMMON IN THE WORLD AND MORAL COURAGE SO RARE.

Mark Twain

IT IS EASY TO BE BRAVE FROM A SAFE DISTANCE.

Aesop

LET BRAVERY BE THY CHOICE, BUT NOT BRAVADO.

Menander

LEARNING

**WHOSO NEGLECTS
LEARNING IN HIS
YOUTH, LOSES THE
PAST AND IS DEAD
FOR THE FUTURE.**

Euripides

I AM ALWAYS READY TO LEARN ALTHOUGH I DO NOT ALWAYS LIKE BEING TAUGHT.

Winston Churchill

IT IS A THOUSAND TIMES BETTER TO HAVE COMMON SENSE WITHOUT EDUCATION THAN TO HAVE EDUCATION WITHOUT COMMON SENSE.

Robert G Ingersoll

EDUCATION IS AN ORNAMENT IN PROSPERITY AND A REFUGE IN ADVERSITY.

Aristotle

A GENTLEMAN NEED NOT KNOW LATIN, BUT HE SHOULD AT LEAST HAVE FORGOTTEN IT.

Brander Matthews

**EDUCATION IS WHEN
YOU READ THE FINE
PRINT. EXPERIENCE
IS WHAT YOU GET
IF YOU DON'T.**

Pete Seeger

SUCCESS

ALWAYS BEAR IN MIND THAT YOUR OWN RESOLUTION TO SUCCEED IS MORE IMPORTANT THAN ANY ONE THING.

Abraham Lincoln

TRY NOT TO BECOME A MAN OF SUCCESS BUT RATHER TO BECOME A MAN OF VALUE.

Albert Einstein

I CAN'T GIVE YOU A
SURE-FIRE FORMULA
FOR SUCCESS, BUT
I CAN GIVE YOU
A FORMULA FOR
FAILURE: TRY TO
PLEASE EVERYBODY
ALL THE TIME.

Herbert Bayard Swope

THE SECRET OF SUCCESS IS SINCERITY. ONCE YOU CAN FAKE THAT YOU'VE GOT IT MADE.

Jean Giraudoux

IF YOU THINK YOU CAN WIN, YOU CAN WIN. FAITH IS NECESSARY TO VICTORY.

William Hazlitt

ADVERSITY

A GEM CANNOT BE POLISHED WITHOUT FRICTION, NOR A MAN PERFECTED WITHOUT TRIALS.

Seneca the Younger

LET US BE OF GOOD CHEER, REMEMBERING THAT THE MISFORTUNES HARDEST TO BEAR ARE THOSE WHICH WILL NEVER HAPPEN.

James Russell Lowell

IF YOU AREN'T IN OVER YOUR HEAD, HOW DO YOU KNOW HOW TALL YOU ARE?

T S Eliot

EVEN IF YOU FALL ON YOUR FACE, YOU'RE STILL MOVING FORWARD.

Robert Gallagher

I'VE DEVELOPED A
NEW PHILOSOPHY ...
I ONLY DREAD ONE
DAY AT A TIME.

Charlie Brown

**IF YOU CAN
FIND A PATH WITH
NO OBSTACLES, IT
PROBABLY DOESN'T
LEAD ANYWHERE.**

Frank A Clark

LUCK

LUCK IS WHAT YOU HAVE LEFT OVER AFTER YOU GIVE 100 PERCENT.

Langston Coleman

SHALLOW MEN BELIEVE IN LUCK. STRONG MEN BELIEVE IN CAUSE AND EFFECT.

Ralph Waldo Emerson

I BELIEVE IN LUCK: HOW ELSE CAN YOU EXPLAIN THE SUCCESS OF THOSE YOU DISLIKE?

Jean Cocteau

DEPEND ON THE RABBIT'S FOOT IF YOU WILL, BUT REMEMBER IT DIDN'T WORK FOR THE RABBIT.

R E Shay

FRIENDSHIP

YOU CAN ALWAYS
TELL A REAL FRIEND:
WHEN YOU'VE
MADE A FOOL OF
YOURSELF HE
DOESN'T FEEL
YOU'VE DONE A
PERMANENT JOB.

Laurence J Peter

IF A MAN DOES
NOT MAKE NEW
ACQUAINTANCES
AS HE ADVANCES
THROUGH LIFE, HE
WILL SOON FIND
HIMSELF ALONE. A
MAN SHOULD KEEP
HIS FRIENDSHIPS IN
CONSTANT REPAIR.

Dr Johnson

TRUE FRIENDS STAB
YOU IN THE FRONT.

Oscar Wilde

**WHEN YOU
CHOOSE YOUR
FRIENDS, DON'T BE
SHORT-CHANGED
BY CHOOSING
PERSONALITY OVER
CHARACTER.**

W Somerset Maugham

ENEMIES

YOU NEVER REALLY KNOW YOUR FRIENDS FROM YOUR ENEMIES UNTIL THE ICE BREAKS.

Eskimo proverb

NEVER INTERRUPT YOUR ENEMY WHEN HE IS MAKING A MISTAKE.

Napoleon Bonaparte

FORGIVE YOUR ENEMIES, BUT NEVER FORGET THEIR NAMES.

John F Kennedy

**EVERYONE NEEDS
A WARM PERSONAL
ENEMY OR TWO
TO KEEP HIM FREE
FROM RUST IN THE
MOVABLE PARTS
OF HIS MIND.**

Gene Fowler

HEALTH

EAT RIGHT, EXERCISE REGULARLY, DIE ANYWAY.

Anon

**IF MAN THINKS
ABOUT HIS PHYSICAL
OR MORAL STATE HE
USUALLY DISCOVERS
THAT HE IS ILL.**

Goethe

WE SHOULD MANAGE
OUR FORTUNE AS
WE DO OUR HEALTH
– ENJOY IT WHEN
GOOD, BE PATIENT
WHEN IT IS BAD,
AND NEVER APPLY
VIOLENT REMEDIES
EXCEPT IN AN
EXTREME NECESSITY.

François de La Rochefoucauld

SEX

**SEX IS A
CONVERSATION
CARRIED OUT BY
OTHER MEANS. IF
YOU GET ON WELL
OUT OF BED, HALF
THE PROBLEMS OF
BED ARE SOLVED.**

Peter Ustinov

SEX ON TELEVISION
CAN'T HURT YOU
UNLESS YOU
FALL OFF.

Anon

THE GOOD THING ABOUT MASTURBATION IS THAT YOU DON'T HAVE TO GET DRESSED UP FOR IT.

Truman Capote

WHERE WOULD MAN BE TODAY IF IT WASN'T FOR WOMEN? IN THE GARDEN OF EDEN EATING WATER MELON AND TAKING IT EASY.

C Kennedy

EXERCISE

IT IS EXERCISE ALONE THAT SUPPORTS THE SPIRITS, AND KEEPS THE MIND IN VIGOUR.

Cicero

I BELIEVE THAT THE
GOOD LORD GAVE US
A FINITE NUMBER OF
HEARTBEATS AND I'M
DAMNED IF I'M GOING
TO USE UP MINE
RUNNING UP AND
DOWN A STREET.

Neil Armstrong

**FIVE DAYS SHALT
THOU LABOUR,
AS THE BIBLE SAYS.
THE SEVENTH DAY IS
THE LORD THY GOD'S.
THE SIXTH DAY IS
FOR FOOTBALL.**

Anthony Burgess

TRAVEL

THE WORLD IS A BOOK, AND THOSE WHO DO NOT TRAVEL READ ONLY A PAGE.

St. Augustine

THE WHOLE OBJECT OF TRAVEL IS NOT TO SET FOOT ON FOREIGN LAND; IT IS AT LAST TO SET FOOT ON ONE'S OWN COUNTRY AS A FOREIGN LAND.

G K Chesterton

A GOOD TRAVELLER HAS NO FIXED PLANS AND IS NOT INTENT ON ARRIVING.

Lao Tzu

WANDERING RE-ESTABLISHES THE ORIGINAL HARMONY WHICH ONCE EXISTED BETWEEN MAN AND THE UNIVERSE.

Anatole France

REFLECTION

IF YOU CAN LOOK
BACK ON YOUR
LIFE WITH
CONTENTMENT,
YOU HAVE ONE
OF MAN'S MOST
PRECIOUS GIFTS
– A SELECTIVE
MEMORY.

Jim Fiebig

IT IS SADDER TO FIND THE PAST AGAIN AND FIND IT INADEQUATE TO THE PRESENT THAN IT IS TO HAVE IT ELUDE YOU AND REMAIN FOREVER A HARMONIOUS CONCEPTION OF MEMORY.

F Scott Fitzgerald

CHERISH ALL YOUR HAPPY MOMENTS; THEY MAKE A FINE CUSHION FOR OLD AGE.

Booth Tarkington

OPPORTUNITY

AN OPTIMIST WILL
TELL YOU THE GLASS
IS HALF-FULL; THE
PESSIMIST, HALF-
EMPTY; AND THE
ENGINEER WILL TELL
YOU THE GLASS IS
TWICE THE SIZE IT
NEEDS TO BE.

Anon

STICK WITH THE OPTIMISTS. IT'S GOING TO BE TOUGH ENOUGH EVEN IF THEY'RE RIGHT.

James Reston

WHEN ONE DOOR CLOSES, ANOTHER OPENS; BUT WE OFTEN LOOK SO LONG AND SO REGRETFULLY UPON THE CLOSED DOOR THAT WE DO NOT SEE THE ONE WHICH HAS OPENED FOR US.

Alexander Graham Bell

THERE IS NO SECURITY ON THIS EARTH; THERE IS ONLY OPPORTUNITY.

General Douglas MacArthur

**GATHER YE
ROSEBUDS WHILE
YE MAY, OLD TIME IS
STILL A-FLYING. AND
THIS SAME FLOWER
THAT SMILES TODAY,
TOMORROW WILL
BE DYING.**

Robert Herrick

NOTHING IS PERMANENT IN THIS WICKED WORLD – NOT EVEN OUR TROUBLES.

Charlie Chaplin

RELAXATION

BESIDES THE NOBLE ART OF GETTING THINGS DONE, THERE IS A NOBLER ART OF LEAVING THINGS UNDONE. THE WISDOM OF LIFE CONSISTS IN THE ELIMINATION OF NONESSENTIALS.

Lin Yutang

**TAKE REST;
A FIELD THAT HAS
RESTED GIVES A
BOUNTIFUL CROP.**

Ovid

THE REAL PROBLEM OF LEISURE TIME IS HOW TO KEEP OTHERS FROM USING YOURS.

Arthur Lacey

**YOUR MIND WILL
ANSWER MOST
QUESTIONS IF YOU
LEARN TO RELAX
AND WAIT FOR
THE ANSWER.**

William S Burroughs

TEMPTATION

**DO NOT WORRY
ABOUT AVOIDING
TEMPTATION. AS YOU
GROW OLDER IT
WILL AVOID YOU.**

Joey Adams

LEAD US NOT INTO TEMPTATION. JUST TELL US WHERE IT IS; WE'LL FIND IT.

Sam Levenson

HOW LIKE HERRINGS AND ONIONS OUR VICES ARE IN THE MORNING AFTER WE HAVE COMMITTED THEM.

Samuel Taylor Coleridge

IF PASSION DRIVES YOU, LET REASON HOLD THE REINS.

Benjamin Franklin

THE FUTURE

THE FUTURE, ACCORDING TO SOME SCIENTISTS, WILL BE EXACTLY LIKE THE PAST, ONLY FAR MORE EXPENSIVE.

John Sladek

CHANGE IS INEVITABLE – EXCEPT FROM A VENDING MACHINE.

Robert Gallagher

WHEN YOU'RE FINISHED CHANGING, YOU'RE FINISHED.

Benjamin Franklin

IT IS A BAD PLAN THAT ADMITS OF NO MODIFICATION.

Syrus

WISDOM

I BELIEVE THAT ALL
WISDOM CONSISTS IN
CARING IMMENSELY
FOR A FEW RIGHT
THINGS, AND NOT
CARING A STRAW
ABOUT THE REST.

John Buchan

WISDOM COMES BY
DISILLUSIONMENT.

George Santayana

**A MAN BEGINS
CUTTING HIS WISDOM
TEETH THE FIRST
TIME HE BITES OFF
MORE THAN HE
CAN CHEW.**

Herb Caen

OLD AGE

MEN DO NOT QUIT PLAYING BECAUSE THEY GROW OLD; THEY GROW OLD BECAUSE THEY QUIT PLAYING.

Oliver Wendell Holmes

THERE IS NO
PLEASURE WORTH
FORGOING JUST FOR
AN EXTRA THREE
YEARS IN THE
GERIATRIC WARD.

John Mortimer

I ADVISE YOU TO GO
ON LIVING SOLELY TO
ENRAGE THOSE WHO
ARE PAYING YOUR
ANNUITIES. IT IS THE
ONLY PLEASURE I
HAVE LEFT.

Voltaire

FIRST YOU FORGET NAMES, THEN YOU FORGET FACES, THEN YOU FORGET TO PULL YOUR ZIPPER UP, THEN YOU FORGET TO PULL YOUR ZIPPER DOWN.

Leo Rosenberg

I THINK I DON'T
REGRET A SINGLE
'EXCESS' OF MY
RESPONSIVE YOUTH
– I ONLY REGRET, IN
MY CHILLED AGE,
CERTAIN OCCASIONS
AND POSSIBILITIES
I DIDN'T EMBRACE.

Henry James

NOTHING IS MORE RESPONSIBLE FOR THE GOOD OLD DAYS THAN A BAD MEMORY.

Franklin Pierce Adams

LIFE

YOUTH IS A BLUNDER; MANHOOD A STRUGGLE; OLD AGE A REGRET.

Benjamin Disraeli

DON'T GO AROUND SAYING THE WORLD OWES YOU A LIVING. THE WORLD OWES YOU NOTHING. IT WAS HERE FIRST.

Mark Twain

DEATH

LIVE AS IF YOU WERE TO DIE TOMORROW. LEARN AS IF YOU WERE TO LIVE FOREVER.

Mahatma Gandhi

HE WHO FEARS DEATH HAS ALREADY LOST THE LIFE HE COVETS.

Cato

OLD AGE ISN'T SO BAD WHEN YOU CONSIDER THE ALTERNATIVE.

Maurice Chevalier

MORE HELP
IS AT HAND...